DEEPWATER VEE

DEEPWATER

~ VEE ~

MELANIE SIEBERT

McCLELLAND & STEWART

LIBRARY AND ARCHIVES CANADA CATALOGUING IN PUBLICATION

Siebert, Melanie
    Deepwater vee / Melanie Siebert.

Poems.
ISBN 978-0-7710-8033-3

I. Title.

PS8637.I25D44 2010   c811.'6   C2009-905149-4

We acknowledge the financial support of the Government of Canada through the Book Publishing Industry Development Program and that of the Government of Ontario through the Ontario Media Development Corporation's Ontario Book Initiative. We further acknowledge the support of the Canada Council for the Arts and the Ontario Arts Council for our publishing program.

Published simultaneously in the United States by McClelland & Stewart Ltd., P.O. Box 1030, Plattsburgh, New York 12901

Library of Congress Control Number: 2009935659

Typeset in Fournier by M&S, Toronto
Printed and bound in Canada

This book is printed on acid-free paper that is 100% recycled, ancient-forest friendly (100% post-consumer waste).

McClelland & Stewart Ltd.
75 Sherbourne Street
Toronto, Ontario
M5A 2P9
www.mcclelland.com

1 2 3 4 5   14 13 12 11 10

✦ *deepwater vee*

A tongue of dark, glassy water that points downstream, indicating a deep channel, a way through whitewater thrown up by riverbed rocks. When running a rapid, these fast, sometimes narrow chutes can be hard to see and tricky to navigate. Threading from V to V is often part instinct, part gamble, part yielding to the water.

CONTENTS

DEEPWATER VEE

CURRENT

On your knees in a boat with sweet rocker and no keel, water pillows up against the red hull with its silt hiss. You sight the drops between boulders, gear and your yeah-buts, your okay-maybes lashed tight, and you heel the canoe on its side for the swift eddy-in, the river's leggy colt-gleam. Spruce reel by, the limestone peaks, skids of outwash. The river sticks a coin behind its ear, pulls two from its wrist.

You've brought food from far away, burned fuel climbing the passes to the Great Divide, ramped, crevassed, the great glacier spilling three ways: Pacific, Arctic, Atlantic. You're taking the low moan of miles home, heading east, northeast, the winded push to the Interior Plains. Even sandstone and the shale beds of the foothills weather in.

River of mixed tongues and guns traded west, frayed edge of the muscle-old herds chewing the hills, fringe between grassland and aspen parkland. The river opaque in all seasons, cartilage, cash flow. When Peter Erasmus first tried the ford, his horse shook him loose and he would've drowned but someone yelled, *Grab her tail*. River of last hunts, the Thirst Dance, the broad forehead of Horsechild, just a boy sweating at his father's side on the long walk to surrender at Carlton in the wolfy breath-heat of the downcast grass.

River, slab of the weathered-down, low under the long hunger, low to the bulked-up meat of the farms, low now, low under the berms of the fat lip. Thick backs of murky sturgeon, sinew of the who-knows-where. And the river slows, gull-flush and scavenging, and you cruise on the gaze of deer, lowrider sliding the afternoon in the valley of the willow of stealth. Opal. Inner wrist of what's left.

You carry water from taps and don't know how to eat what's here. You haven't built your boat, still you take a bearing in the magnetic field of runoff, beam your signals to the satellites of fallen birds. And this boat grafts you to water's big-winged glide, its giveaway, the cool salve of its going-going-gone, pushing to a wavering long-held note. Inner wrist, underworld. Water on the downgrade, flowing loaded and filmed.

— *North Saskatchewan River*

DEEPWATER VEE

Water slants its root into your gill-surfaced ride and you steal the inside
of the Devil's Elbow, miss the ledges, narrowly, take the downstream
tongue, deepwater vee funnelled to a wavetrain piling around the bend.
You play out converging currents, sloppy haystacks curling
over the gunwales, less and less freeboard, bailing
on the fly—bygone and softly blistered,
weighted here. A cougar wades in, tail high and swatting,
swims across your bearing down. And bees go to the balsam
poplar for resin to waterproof their hives, and the river
smooths its stride, gold haunches of two elk
darkening into the bush.

Hunter rises in your throat.

Sweep by.

~

The sun, an engine two-stroking way off in the distance,
North Sask, now a muddy adagio, cowhide, slack, wobbling
with the too-slow-vibrato of the sundown hills.
This river takes other rivers in its mouth.
Your mouth to its mouth.
The other rivers of your mouth.
Your mouth to its mouth.
The other rivers of the mouth.
Other rivers braiding the mouth.

~⟨⟩

Alexander Mackenzie chews drymeat.
Chews and chews the tough meat, rapid of the not-yet drowned.
Fort Chipewyan, 1794, sitting out the winter, useless now, and sitting
in the dark, trying to make a copy of his journal, record of his journey
cross-continent, derailed down the Deh Cho, big river that bull-headed
north, whipped him 1,600 miles north and back again before he could hack
a way over the squall-cuffed mountains to the west.
                                                And now he sits. Chewing.
Chewing the black-spruce steepled dark, ramparts of the narrows
slumping down, tumpline neck muscle, burning-out lamp
at the back of his chewing, scow lurching over the ledges, taking on
water, taking on the brawling water, going down, going down.

This is where the hunters leave him.
The men who've put meat in his mouth.

They can't carry him now.
The mounds of his hands, the Precambrian
mounds of his hands on the table.
He doesn't get a word down.
All winter. Chewing the old meat.

And Kitty? Where is Kitty now?
The bow spray of her three-rivers lips.

Darkness sways in, feathered earring, stretched lobe.
Bent to water, cows in soft focus lift their eyes to your passing,
their hooves sunk in, the banks trampled. You stray-sail
the evening, sun-loaded, belly full, feet up on the gunwales.
The river ruffles with the leftover wind of an unnamed
star that explodes into a supernova. Chinese astronomers,
1054, tilt their heads to calculations, and on the prairies
someone carves the ruptured star on a stone
next to the crescent moon. Traffic on the valley crest,
glinting beyond earshot, loitering to Saskatoon.
Something of a tease, the river twists
your boat in the back and forth of almost
nothing: pair of shoes dangling from a power line,
whistle made from a blade of grass, beginner
violin recital, *Twinkle, Twinkle,* seedheads
bobbing on the stalk, wavering bow-arm arcs.

River, slow, shambling, smelling like grain
trucked over the steep icy grade on the Emerson Trail,
door open, one foot on the running board
in case the rig slides, ditches six-feet deep, full of water.
Grandfather spitting black all the way back from the smutty grain.
Bear liver frying over the fire.
Sleeping under the truck.

River's trucker mouth, lumber hauled
for the Pinto Creek sawmill across the Wapiti south of Wembley.
Winter hits.
Holes drilled into the ice.
Timbers stood upright and frozen in.
Cross pieces nailed to the poles, two uneven tracks, planks
laid across the river. Loads sway over.

~⟩

Overburden, Athabasca muskeg, stripped back.
400-ton heavy-haulers dump-trucking the boreal forest.
The oil-slick mirrors of the tar ponds, seen from space,
blown pupils, looking/not-looking, ragging
    down, slugback
        seep into porewater.

Mike says right from grade ten you've got the smack for oil and driving
your own truck.

His uncle was the Chief, fifteen years ago, who canoed out, scooped up
four bottles of water, and took it to Ottawa to see if they would drink it.

And the Fort Chip man who flies out 200 pounds of pickerel riddled
with tumours, bulging eyes, crooked tails, and pushed-in faces to the
government, finds out they were left in a truck to rot.

A woman from Black Lake keeps a list of the dead in her spiral notebook.

Mike cuts his hair.

~)

The river draws its map from memory,
plots its waypoints on your wingspan:
Wind of the old black-and-white photos of baptisms
down by Petrofka bridge, water at the backs of knees,
girls' skirts swimming up, white shirts,
father, son, and holy muddy water.

Wind of the fishhook wheeled into the thick
of his palm. Grandfather, methodical, bows his head,
takes the pliers and pushes the hook through, clips the barbs,
and sends it sailing back. Wind of the letter he finds from his wife
after she's passed on, what she couldn't say any other way.

Wind streamers, wind of the snow swooping out of the black,
blowing all the way from when you drove ambulance,
transfer from P.A. to Saskatoon, almost halfway, Hwy 11,
middle night, slow going over hard drifts,
your partner in the rearview hatch of warm light,
taking vitals, bent over a clipboard.
The girl seemed to float when lifted on the bottom sheet
from hospital bed to stretcher, ventilator slushing rhythmic,
gold paint around her mouth from the spray can.
Attempted. NOK: unknown. No clues on the tripsheet
where she was found or by whom, just that she's from Duck Lake
and when you drive past, though you can't see a thing, you wish
you could turn off on a road that would take her home.
Helpless, you've not been trained in how to be helpless.

Mackenzie winters in the hip of the wounded red deer.

And the dream hoof-pounds northwest by west for ice-choked
miles, then further north into the swollen ankles of the unending
coldrush, hip-high current, northwest by west then further north,
the bloodworking haunch of the wounded deer, whirlpools of wild
onions mixed with pemmican, smoke-riding the tar of his lips.

The river still running under the ice,
  the river blowing on the wound,
    the river, gun-muzzle burst in his hand.

The under-river, the greased axles of the waydown river,
hundreds of metres below the river and kilometres wide, flowing
through preglacial sediments, through smallest
pores, the shy birds of its below-the-radar
first violins, the volts of its silver
pins-and-needles porewater.
Its tai chi empty hand, single
whip, slow now, outwash
undersound.

North Sask wobbles into the underbrush voice box.
Acid rain trucks in from the tar sands.
Two weeks ago stormwater
overflowed sewage into the river.
Vultures tip twitchy on dihedral wings,
for days now you've seen no one in this valley.
Water's dropped, shoals showing
and in the evening you wade in, knee deep
and then a little deeper, lie back,
what the hell, heels digging in.

Sleep with spilled river-down skin,
sound of a bird in the coyote's mouth.

You can't drink this water.
You can't drink this water.

BELLANCA ESKER

66° 21' 35" N
110° 06' 47" W

The clouds hurtle overhead and you boat the parched ground. Parched
    ground water-laid and wolfing east. The heart that sprawls
       horizon to horizon is the good roof.
The heart, a den, dug in, marked
by piss and prickly saxifrage, dark opening
in the esker's muscled flank. And the slow pan—
      far slope to far slope, clouds muskox-skulled and bossing in,
the heart stomaching all this sky, light ramming
thunderheads in the west, and in the east, soundless, shadowless,
sweeps of virga, rain that falls but never pelts the barrens.
Bending like the aimless, yielding stems,
        the heart, blown to the ground.

—— *Burnside River*

ALSEK LAKE

59° 11' 06" N
138° 10' 38" W

I wake ancient in the night, ice-kicked, hunkered down
under the thunder-flask, glaciers calving bergs,
drop-boiling three miles away. Rough-tongued,
relentless, the waves trundle in, bucking
the ear's long-handled boom. Bowl of a lake,
scummed with ten thousand years of ice. The chest
caves open, glacial ages roll over,
become drinkable. Drink this:
each breath a fist, each fist a hobo,
useless and forgettable.
Listen under,
                    way under the thick-slabbed bawl—
the ear picks up tiny-tiny
wasp-winged
            spit-sizzle,
ice shatter,
                chipping
        hits of unpolluted
            air.

                        —— *Tatshenshini / Alsek River*

BRIDGE TO SHELL'S ALBIAN MINE,
DOWNSTREAM, RIVER RIGHT

57° 08' 07" N
111° 36' 28" W

We were taking samples of water, four inches below the surface.
We stashed suspended sediments on ice in a cooler,
shift change high-strung and booming over the bridge.
We wanted to know what was coming down the feeders,
the Horse, the Steepbank, the Hangingstone,
the Firebag, etc., what was going discreet
and malignant. Our shirts hung loose, we were occupied
      by a valley.
Buddy Wasisname and the Other Fellas selling tickets hundred bucks
a pop in Fort Mac, mixed-bag down-home entertainment, bumper-
to-bumper, weather, landscape, and coke-ovened kickbacks,
semi-hungover, we ripped a vinyl mattress out of the mud.
The foam churned up, clung to our shins, the Mackenzie
Delta, far off and hovering with the luminosity of film,
long radio antenna flexing on top of a truck.
                We still packed
our own airstrips, stacked pallets, the theme of voyeurism
waterproof with our lunches. We joked, slightly sweaty,
groundwater heating up, in situ. In the drainage ditch,
in the standing-room-only quarry of the ancestors
waiting for its nuclear reactor, we floated so easily
and alien, notched, open-pit, microblades and spear points
layered up, the creeks creeking in, not everything measured
in bathtubs, football fields, and Olympic-sized swimming pools.
        We were dusty, cutback,

                    wearing latex gloves and stammering
100 ml samples of water. The dykes leaked secret agreements.
We weren't replaying big-screen emotions when
                                        whitecaps came up.
The river rode its stolen bikes, serial numbers filed off.

                        —— *Athabasca River*

BUSKER

—For my brother

8th Ave. / Centre St.

Coat sewn out of ropes of odd lengths and diameters.
Tangled, frayed, sleeves not quite long enough.
Coat worn to conduct the choir of the after-hours, the fists-
not-yet-flying choir. Smoke and coins chucked in the offering plate.
Sweat-soaked coat, dragging the salted streets coat, knotted-up
coat, what could have been, what could have been.
Blue-bitten stars chewed into his inner cheeks.
Buttons, missing. Pockets gritty, matchbooks,
butts, quarters, a few spare parts for his sax.
Horn raised to the lips, the moist reed.
He strings slow notes, snare wires, salvage
or salvation, maybe not in this life.
Warm breath fogs the bell.
It's raining, street empty,
wrists bare.

BUSKER

Heading east on 9th

He follows signs: Coke truck chatters a manhole lid, yanks his head in the direction of downtown, red is risk but Coke is it, better follow, fists open in his pockets, he flips a buck and gets five back flapping on the sidewalk, he takes the wake behind some lady who blares hey-you and jaywalks across traffic, parking meter jumps, time's up, two straws in a pop can balanced on a ledge, two and an edge signals second chance, green is go, and the walk-lights blink: walk on, walker.

He walks, flares a flame cauldron, 50-gigajoules/hr gas-mind at the top of the Calgary Tower, its sway to the alley jazz club, alley for alice, alice in under-land, under-band playing a bargain-basement remand. He walks in, bearded and thirsty.

Right place at the right time. Orders coffee, tips five. The jam band jams a hair on the tongue, piano skates on repeat, guitar and bass trucking easy. He listens, listens hard to the bottled, to the trumped-up, to the walls sweating close, head in his hands. It's the hour of sharps. He waits and waits, papery, striated, waspnest, waits for a sign, until the piano sits empty while the other players play on. His breath in the cup smells animal.

When he's pulled to the stage, he walks wary and creased, circles around by the sidewall, then bends over the piano like someone stooping over a puddle to drink clear water off the top. He's been told: play with the keeled-over loveliness of those who have given in for the night, packed up, moved on, moved out, wrists smooth as willows. The drums hunch under a horn solo. The piano has eyeteeth. He's shedding layers, stoking the changes, handling the sweet, slow-burning keys. The pour-over phrases wash out the bar lines, the crawlspace under the lowest note bears down humid and thick, a plague of frogs in the ditches. And a breeze skiffs in, the night a good night, damn good, whiskered and licking the salt off his palms.

SURF CITY

61° 52' 31" N
126° 38' 42" W

Water's summer-toned muscle funnels under hip-
tilt held midstream by breakwater falling
down the wave face. Kite-boat flown
on the fat trem of a ringing chord,
bilgewater piling in.
Smooth dune,
one debt forgiven,
lamp inside a pouring pitcher,
surf wave bulges like a new earth born.
Perhaps you've foiled death by eating this flower.

⸺ Churchill River

MACKENZIE'S DREAM

He has tromped the grease trail with two pistols under his belt,
hacked a road for commerce through the hot flank of the fleeing deer,
been warned to go no farther and carried on.
All this time he has travelled unwounded.
But when the dream comes, it comes pounding
in the hydraulic drowning machine of his hip.
Thirty-two years old, Mackenzie drills into the unfuelled offshore
throat, dull knife at the first joint, rocks falling from the cliffs like rifle
shots, black box of sky lowered down, tattered Lake of the Hills
frozen now and lapping in his hip, ailing and suddenly old.
Everyone knows he's leaving and won't be back.
Kitty, his woman, his northwest woman, taken
under his furs, taken and held, Kitty
drops a long-distance gallop over her face, gaining speed,
seeds her flashing hands in the stinking rich floodplain.
Mackenzie hard-rides his own bad breath alone into the gritting
rachet, winter-jacked dream, hauling the scow
of the dead. He takes the rope slung over his shoulder,
the coals of that rope in his hands, the weight of his body
lashing into the pull, the thirst of the rope, the hard strobe
of rope, its cut diamonds in the mane of his bleeding hands.
He is drunk now and oiled to the floor.
The letters he burns fly up with the wings of owls.
What does he love? What does he love now in this secret
grave where wind grouses under all things?
Thick tar of the hills pounding in his spoils.

CHOKER

62° 41' 44" N
129° 15' 16" W

Scout from river-right of small gravel island if enough
water, no sneak route.

Tricky line.
Well, no line.
Walrus-rocks bulked up
and belching. Many-pronged
hello current, hello nightshift wits
going vascular, unmended.
Kissed a lot of good lips.
Poachers.
Rock-strobes.
Fly buzz, liquored
rock-bloom, hull
crackers.

—— *South Nahanni River*

BUSKER

15 Ave. SE / 1 St. SE, second-storey corner room

One chair, uneven legs.
Moth under an overturned glass.
Hammer, bag of nails, and a cranked back.
Night bearings, out-of-round, pitted and spalling,
occasional sirens. Not quite silence, but standstill's
ampule, making do, brown glass snapped at the neck,
pushed slow—not a drug, just the wait-it-out—good to pull
the whole night. The following instant,

                                        ballast.

The next,
              moving sledge.
Shoulder socket divines a miles-away downpour.
Next, habitual chin-ups in a doorway.
He puts the moth in a film canister
to deliver to the night. Half-mast,
confessing nil, in a room
lit by choppy light from out-the-window
unknown source, in the cargo-hold hum of upgraders
putting out, he hears nothing.
Limitation aspires to purity.
This silence piles its pile of bills.

SKULL CANYON

56° 46' 22" N
109° 23' 27" W

*"If I should lose all faith in God, I think I should continue
to believe invincibly in the world."*
                                        —Pierre Teilhard de Chardin

Mass and gravity at their holy work, you're held
                              under,
under aerated, scrap-heap, burning-bush water,
back to the polished rock-slide, the oceangoing
prop-wash, PFD not rated for a Maytag
mind, semi-buoyant, debris on epinephrine,
hydraulic jump bucked from the drop,
bottom-trawler scrolling black-and-white
reel-to-reel, path you'd never choose,
lungs, two pistons of a pitch-dark flyway,
pumping for lift, lugging
              water.
Only owls hear mice move under snow.

                              —— *Clearwater River*

UNNAMED CREEK

62° 39' 57" N
104° 44' 12" W

Belly down in a shallow bowl where wind lies stretchmarked and idling,
hinting at the bottle in your hand. The other animals hidden, cloaked
in a thicker wind. They've left vagrant trails across the split-open
fruit of the hills. You're brittle here, brittle and old as lichen.
The smell of decay rides its ship over the edge of the world.
Terns pour their dye into the wind and show you its limber lines.
Your lungs, swinging doors, your pretty rags, grass seeds
blown into fox tracks.

—— Thelon River

BUSKER

Macleod Trail / 17, heading west

Another ridge-walk down the close-captioned night. Main street on shuffle. He's fuelling freebie mashed potatoes and talking into the black box that records crucial minutes popping in the ears. Everything's under construction. Or destruction, depending. Turbulence minimal, down-drift of the tonal range, day-breathers, he reports, have turned in at the milk hotel. He'll walk to city limits, maybe back. Kids still lift the dance floors. Downtown falls behind him like plastic cutlery and a drowsy row of bees. The footings, poured. Sky's a new roof hung by a crane exerting unauthorized effort at this late hour.

MACKENZIE'S DREAM

Mackenzie stilts up on the ammunition of his own spindly legs,
veers in huge, no-bullshit strides. Head butting, horn display.
Wildfire on stilts, swaying, methodical, fatigued and without
a kill. The dream chuffs in his ear, an old bear.
He rides up over the land, lucky undershirt,
strong back chafing tanker clouds, private parts covered.
Spread like a map, the land, lines sketched in
      but twitchy, uncertain.
            Terrain in a-fib, with or without angina.
Bribes grease his lope, his long-legged, drill-rig gait.
And the dream swelters downwash, the boot-to-the-head
bladebeat of his stride, animals flee
in all directions. The land, small and aimless,
      a pitching boat
miles under his feet, pinpricks of scurrying
at hundred-year-old campsites. People rattling
    after the animals, the ripe flags of nations
      glued to the underside of the wind.
      Flank-to-flank heat.
Mackenzie kicks open doors and enters by the mouth,
dogshead back to half-cock, black powder in the flashpan.
River cranks its flywheel in his head.
He's nauseous now and can't feel the ground.
One hand staunches a hindquarter wound,
udder full of milk, the other bangs
      the river open and shut. The clattering
knives, beads, awls, flints, hatchets, fire-steals,

fly off the edge of the shifty world.

He could chart this too—wobbling ankles, the slouch
of a mouth without orders, wet gunpowder spread on the ground.

In the dream,

bare-headed, lock-jammed.

His stride goes ragged as a firemoth.

On the third day of hunger it is hard to walk
far or fast enough to kill. White iron

pack ice bulges in the distance.

GRANDMOTHER

—To Cornelia Siebert (1920–1999)

We went on unanswered, unanswered and astray. We went on staying awake at the kitchen table, lifting mugs of a good yield with eczema hands, lifting the sod of what could have been morning. We went on in the erasing wind, topsoil blowing away, the windbreak flimsy, poplars bent, blown through, plumed with dirt that was leaving. We went on chemicalled and overflowing. We went on roughshod. We went on whatsoever. Bring your psalms down, down to the ground.

We went on sparrowed, thin-boned and lifting in all directions. We went on without a mothertongue, without needing a mothertongue. We went on with seeds rigged to be sterile. We pulled our scarves from the hills, unravelled our eyes, pried the door off the dirt. We went on not saying, not saying anything. Wings were the cargo we carried on. Letters from the ocean scrubbed into the floor. We went on in the flood-lights, in the trigger-finger fix-fix-fix crescendo of the makeshift.

GRANDMOTHER

You were huffing ambulance oxygen and a cold spell
sloped off your neck, your migration, slipshod
and unspoken, buckshot sprayed wide,
sky hardening down to tarmac where you were lugging
supper to the field, over and over, steaming meals,
squall line fishtailing west, runoff, washboard grid and water
on the lungs. Lifting your skirts, stepping into a boat,
the gunwhale tipped to your weight and sloshed back.
Untested weapons cruised the boreal valley.
You were blue-lipped, jacking up your mud-wet, acidic
hems and Cheyne-Stoking the highwater mark, sky now ribboned glass
where an IV swung above your head on the fast corners, feet swelling.
You were warming milk every morning in a pan for the cats.
A bear ripped into the freezer.
It dragged its entrails, wound itself round and round a tree.
We chased escaped bison on dirtbikes, poured
dirty oil on the driveway to keep the dust down.
We were going to choir practice on Wednesdays, learning our parts,
hauling goods for good money north to build a new blacktop.
We shovelled seed grain from truck to boxcar,
food banks and immune systems revved to the redline.
Flare stacks burned off the pressure.
One arsenic plume ghosted 1,200 feet in fifteen years.
Your knees were wet and I thought you would look back.
We had heard that the wing rolls up when the weapon is dropped.
I thought you would braid your voice into the gridlock, low-lying
weather, a rope tied to the handle of a pail, to our sleep,
hard and nosedown, pooled under fur-bearing animals,
hailed-out windows, under the heat-sink of a CANDU reactor.

HELL ROARING CREEK

61° 52' 31" N
126° 38' 42" W

Maybe, he says, the body is buoyed up
by a force equal to the weight
of what's been displaced.
We're talking erosion
and forgiveness. Silt load
a foot thick, swamps the dryas flats,
dropped by the creek that boots a shifty ditch
through the water-moved plain, now woollen and doped.
In the tent, we miss the valley fog's
lynx prowl, its soft-pedalled synth pads.
The topo, he says, has this creek mislabelled.
Three valleys back, the Secret Lakes pour their stiff drinks.
When we look out, trees, cliffs,
epochs of buckled crust have disappeared.
The softbox nightlight, swollen
and cried out, floats us in creek sound,
damp scent of yarrow and spruce bark,
big hooves floundering up a siltbank,
creek lifting what it can,
till sleep bears up its load.

— *South Nahanni River*

BUSKER

10th Ave., across from the rail yards

Certain riffs are street riffs, meant for open air, he thinks. The more indifferent the crowd the sweeter they sound, as if meant for no one. Good music—sly and lived-in as the wind. But when the street's snowed under and dark lumbers in, he hawks his sax and guitar for a little heat pumped into his apartment and a couple packs of cigarettes. Just enough to get him through until he can sell the rest and buy a ticket to somewhere where the streets are sweaty and music-slick.

The piano's what he plays in winter. Jazz is different when it's breathed than when it's hammered out through the fingers. The piano a black grand, a big animal, a big god, denned but not sleeping. Across his empty room it sits. Phlegmed-up, coal-shouldered, barely breathing.

All dishes have been broken, cups, plates, bowls, anything that could function as an ashtray he's broken. Out the window on the roof, he's piled the white ceramic pieces like a collection of punched-out teeth. Window open or window closed, the constant debate. He wants to shut out the city-whine, the side-swiping snow. But the wind—

Sure, he could knock down some discordant chords, jam the syncopation, thick like after-crying shudders, his nail-bitten right hand skidding a melody like the faintest wind on skin. Or he could sit with his wind-whipped goner-dreams, leg slung over his knee, crow-tapping his mid-air foot, beaking out the unplayed rhythm, body hunched as if against the black curl of earth. Or he could crawl through the window onto the roof, stand completely still, only his hand moving the smooth arc to his lips. When he smokes on the roof edge, the city smoulders below.

GRASS HILLS, RIVER LEFT, DOWNSTREAM OF BATTLEFORD

52° 30' 11" N
107° 43' 47" W

We move like bulky animals on the frayed rope
of horizon, pitch our scent downstream,

build a fire in the sand, strum
a pawnshop guitar in our rented stadium.

North Sask lowballs by. Light, its guesswork,
rigs another stage and nothing comes down for a drink.

When Glenn films Big Bear's dream for CBC,
camera one shoots close-up dirt smoking from the hooves.

Cowboys stampede thirty buffalo into a last-second veer, lens-
stutter, breathstop. Camera one licks dust off his lips.

Thirty buffalo cut-and-paste into hundreds, hundreds
on-screen pitching into the hole of the ground.

Soft hide of the sky flaps overhead. The herds gone.
Tonight we find a boulder in an old bowl of dirt, granite

rubbed smooth, big heat, oils, heavy bodies leaned into rock.

— North Saskatchewan River

GRANDMOTHER

We said the dead were flown, lifted to a sure life,
the body sloughed off, and we went on
measuring parts per million, underwater
grease rags still throatsinging river's crankshafts,
ruffed grouse drumming in our lower backs,
bent to water, waving a hydrophone wired to pick up
the mythic toothed gears, the signal now frying
static, funnel clouds mounting stolen goods and letting loose.
We went on far-flung, we went on washed-out bridges.
Silence silted in—sand-seep from the walls of a cold house,
our religion, the forgetting we have had to profess,
ghost forest in the reservoir, poor insulation,
red inner lining of my wet eiderdown.
A bee will chew a hole in the side of a closed flower.
Cribbed well, a hotbed made with storm windows,
the human heart can be cradled in a metal device
that keeps it warm and beating. And we went on
100,000 pounds of river bottom dredged, intercostal
muscles heaving damped sound, slurried underwater
sound, pillowed mounds, dredged
and still slumping in.

THE LIMIT OF TRAVELS IN THIS DIRECTION

The dream that's not a dream stings in the teeth
of Mackenzie's momentum, fish-oiled hair, double-or-nothing
quad burn going shaky. Doused fires limp the shores.
Thick fog descends, flesh of boiled trout, a bone ladle.
All bullets sunk in the river,
                              every direction, no direction.
The feverish and sick push off in boats,
too weak to steer or paddle, laid in the hold.
                    Canoes aerosol in the current,
              twist in the guard hairs of a diffuse, weakling sun,
                drizzle syringes the lips.
Impossible to take a reading now.
                              The book of observation
blank as the Stinking Lake, subsoil of drunk-tank light
that floats the lost in the waterlogged territory.
The only cache, blood shunted to the core,
the dead salted in their inwardness.
                    Wrists,
                    weights on the gunwales,
fingertips skating water,
              every hour, the last hour. The fat
blisters on a fire without heat,
wasps at the thin-skinned
                    windowpane,
                              the body shedding
origins, spending its last energy, prying

aimless into fog for the dim

                    shift of what could be land.

      Apnea

      then another breath.

           Apnea

BUSKER

Hwy 63, Grassland to Fort Mac, under construction

First snow starts. Stops. Starts.
Distance disappears, perpetual
dispersal. He picks bottles in the ditch,
in the fuzzy longshot of a pinhole camera,
upside-down migration, losing light.
Twelve bears shot at an unfenced dump.
Oil posts another loss.
Snow blanks out the signs.
Unscheduled, iffy.
Each axle pays out spindrift in his downy ear.

MACKENZIE, HAVING NOT SEEN
A STAR SINCE LEAVING ATHABASCA

Scanning all night, nor could he bend it,
calculations, fully unpardonable, land looms by trick light,
fractal islands or shore, boiling, skittish
magnetic variation, boots worn through in a day.
Brewed 24-hour sun, cold-cocked,
cursed thistle,
        augurs the 360-
degree swing, indiscriminate, owing rotgut,
pitch pressed into the split,
stone in a sling, never solvent.
                    Wind bronchials the same
                    quarter. Past a hundred cold cook fires.
Lat/long skewed, volatile, nerve-knots hissing in the armpits.
Needle grinds into the ground's swell.

BUSKER

payphone, unknown location

You want to stink like this? You want to see weather get stormy? You want dirt rammed up your nostrils and the contour lines of your brain mapped on a machine that's wired to show you're fucked? You want a bunk where you can vomit in private? You want some virgins and their lamps to come and deck this place out? You want to have babies and have them pawed at and pawing back, you want them to go to church every Sunday and eat every pea off their plates? You want to grind your ankles against each other, grind your knees against each other, and fetal-up for six hours of footsteps past your head? You want to hack the tails off your dreams and sell them for a buck a piece? You want to bend over and lick ants off the stones, hunker down in a hole and crack the toes of scrawny dogs to get at the last bits of marrow? You want to pitch-slather your split lips? You want your fingers in the frost-broke pavement, you want to dig your fingers into the storm drains? You want the stones to roll over and show their bellies, their scarred little bellies, is that what you want?

SHIFTING, OVERRUN, THE SYMPTOMS, THE SHOALS BUILDING

The mouth digs a deep ditch. It'll sprawl here for centuries, maybe longer. You could wear dark glasses but the mouth has no disguise. It sleeps days out in the open, glossy as a lake, wasted, tailings. Propane-cannons batter the air where birds still glide down to the oily surface.

~)

Whosoever knows starlight dwarfed by coke stacks blowing off the volatiles, whosoever wheels through the embers of the after–3 a.m. city, whosoever opens the pub door opens into a choir of low womanly notes. The smokeless smoke. You could say they're all thinner now, leaning weedy and wicking fuel. Hands twitchy as flies on the windowsill. If a stranger surfs you flowers and a wink, then disappears, toast to paranoia, to barbs or bad decibels, to getting out of here, to a fire-escape conversation with the raining ash.

~)

Even the lightest touch of a hand, a blow. Axe head shoved onto the splintering handle and left in a bucket to soak. The wood swells. The axe swung over a shoulder, carried out, leaned against the ATCO trailer.

~)

Peninsula of cracked stone. The brine that leaches through pores. The hee-haw Geiger-countered distance, here to there, and back. How to get back.

Try to explain to the hospital's armed guards a brain ripped by seismic lines.

~)

Lie back. Pike-slick and double-jawed. Yanked here, left to rot.

Lie back stung. Stupid and scaled like stadium lights. Tumoured, watery. Funnelled sun, a stone in the gullet.

D'AOUST ESKER

62° 44' 01" N
104° 44' 45" W

We burn a small fire of survey stakes.
Burn and stare, Adam's ribcage wedged open.
The sky puts on weight. Clouds heave in, scarred
dark, bear-loping east, big chests
blazed and heavy as gunny sacks of uranium ore.

We're fatherless here.
The way-back lake bubbles radon.
We're unsure if we can drink the water,
but do. But do.

— *Thelon River*

NADLOK—PLACE WHERE THE DEER CROSS

66° 16' 03" N
110° 14' 45" W

Water lapping still without this year's floating hair,
the coming hair, where the shallows are paved with bone
and the river bothways goes lax, where it murmurs
gun-shy, in its gauze an island of cutting floors,
where a woman has sewn the windskin to the waterskin,
where she takes her time chewing down the old bones, the dug-up
bones, three hundred years of caribou hunted in the pang
of the Little Ice Age. She's putting flour in the bins of the wind,
where a fox sleds the horizon like the stirred tallow sun, where hills already
pound, the hills in their old-cow heat, the caribou coming, soon coming
from the wind-rucked lakes, from Ghost Lake, Dry Bones Lake,
Lake of the Enemy, up Snare Lake to Winter Lake, sleeting
over the hardpack of Starvation Lake to Lac de Gras, the antlered
sprawl of Kathawachaga, Contwoyto, steaming up from the freeze-thaw
flanks of the Coppermine, the Tree, and the Hood, from the blueslope
sundogs and the bunkers of winter wolves with an inch of rump fat,
caribou tasting like spruce in the ice-knife spring, caribou coming
nervy and buoyant, coming winter-rank into the hot ears of helicopters
and the blow-smoke of a century, coming roaded and dazed, their dark
circled eyes, ice rot, drill noise, the deep port of the coming heat,
where a woman waits, her needles stashed in the leg bones of geese,
where a woman waits and will do what she has to, when she has to—
she'll rip the seam and the caribou will pour
from the sac of the watersky.

— Burnside River

45

MAP UNROLLED ON THE TABLE

We're plotting in the spate of symbols.
I track poorly now, 500 tons of water
every minute in loose slacks. The description of the land
in an early report infects the description of the land in a later report.
But tell me the aspen aren't clumsy and wicking
bright kerosene against the black spruce curtains.
According to Mary PeeMee, Horsechild, twelve years old, follows
his father secretly deep into the muskeg-stunted bush.
I add, he licks the scratches on his arms.
The way he puts his feet down, he knows something
about death. Blunt scent rubbed on trees.

We're dead reckoning from the last ballparked position fix—
Flocks of pigeons that eclipsed the sun.
Fishy heaps of crushed iridescent cars.
Pipelines knifing the territories.
Dragonfly wings ticking apart in a wind.
The promise I made re: confidentiality.
Traffic and the noise of traffic.
Something sworn in to the six-foot-high grass.

~)

Annealing all materials into malleable materials,
for five centuries European mapping conventions heat-cool
heat-cool spatial equivalence. Surface of the paper/land,
big-brained alloy with oddball properties.

Arrowsmith charts the Interior on Mercator's projection,
etches light-sensitive tissues, info trickling in,
cascade of chemical and electrical events. All interactions
heavily mediated by air and water and bales of super abundance.
Trust this. The map pays out a bristling rope.
The blank spaces will be filled in or will remain blank,
slow waves of the Rockies crashing against the Interior Plains.

All maps are meals served with salt and good wine.
My blinds are pulled. Pine hangs 180 nautical miles offshore,
while Mackenzie's house fire melts down instruments.
I can smell it.
A passenger pigeon's eyes sewn shut
with needle and thread before it's tethered to a stool.
The flocks that fog in to its distress, batted so easily out of the air.
Easily, the average river takes a million years to move a grain of sand
100 inches. Map turned scrim, opaque, not lit from behind.

~◠

You can walk a long way upstream
when the river is at its lowest and blunder
on the withheld rations.
Horsechild is just one man,
runt rabbit slung over his shoulder,
walking the tight perimeter of the surveyed land.
He is unfaithful on just one occasion.
He picks up the beads sprayed from his neck, every one,
on hands and knees, holds them loose in his hands,
bear's paw loose in his hands.
Mary PeeMee takes no other.
Swimming beads in an enamel saucer.
She's staring out the window at the pollen-roped windshift.

I have a concentric desolate feeling.
I have a sandbar building its ghost below the surface of the water.
I have an artificial horizon, a shallow tray filled with mercury.
Little tacks fix hand-drawn maps to the bloody winds.
And I only have five senses.
When the air is wet, the scent picks up.
A train derails, pigeons rot in their cages.
I'm drinking you under the table.

Europa climbs over Jupiter's shoulder
in the scope of a clear night. Do the calculation.
Your position fixed by a mathematical model.
Water always on the move even at record lows.
Photography here is dull like the map is dull.
The magnetic field creeps westward,
wings pinned in a different place each night.
Can you feel it?

So what. The sandbar willows build their cities with narrow streets.
On an island in the Saskatchewan, hilltop breezy and stung
with crushed grass, Horsechild hides next to his father.
Soldiers steamboat past and set camp 100 yards downstream.
Bacon smell floats up.

Night rolls, domed, loupe to the eye.

The motor stalls upstream of Deadhead Corner
and the water taxi man fiddles with the gas line.
We drift sideways in the sudden quiet,
silt skidding off aluminum,
one dry-split paddle, one 2x4 to steer,
16-foot deadheads twanging in the current.

My main concern is the discontinuation of psychological care.
Jackknifing the nerve ends.
Over-exposed half-sleep loosening the tracking stars.
Sinking into muskeg.
A stuttered underbreath, the image blown
bright and invisible, hair that drips from the fingers.
All maps report gunfire.

Horsechild brings food to the prisoners in the Stony Mountain Pen.
His father knows how to evaporate from his cell, can ride
all day on a steamy mare, bear's claw at his throat, skimming
the backs of the stampeding hills.

The boy holds out bannock and an extra boiled pork rind.

Without effort, as if I'm underwater, lit
windows swim like walleye eyeshine.
The City has erected floodlights at the weir
where its uniform ledge spills a keeper.
I'm afraid to go home.
Pelicans sail in slowly, a breathspan above the current,
for good fishing on the boil line and a strong eddy
that conveyor-belts them up to the foaming edge.
If he has used a good rope.
If he has dressed the knots neatly.
If a sound like wings has flown his mouth
and flaps in the corners of the shrinking room.

I heave up into the truck like climbing into a purring, hydraulic, special-effects sky.

I haul throbbing temples from the Baldface Hills.

I haul a part-time moodswing to the ferry, to the river and its overturned pianos.

Under the influence of day-flying owls and a century or so, I haul psychological assessments to build up the townsite.

Take off the boomers, throw the engine into reverse, jam the brakes, and send the load skidding off.

Wait for midnight frost to harden the outlook, a good deal on bottle nipples to keep the spark plugs dry.

I split rocks with a crowbar to build a road past Medicine Lake.

I tip the dayshift/nightshift on its side, wheels left spinning, wetrot brewing in the box.

When the meat goes off, I add more onions.

Really, a man sits on a crane hook 500 feet above the riverbed at the dam site. He's getting paid for that ride.

A mechanic throws a match down on the wet cement and the uninsured projections burn in the garage.

I shovel until my back is poor, pour rivers into large basins, drink the cream straight.

Every night I wash myself in a little stream that hauls through the snow.

I am also other than what I haul on a daily basis.

On a ladder, in the second-hand light, I pull my legs across rotten ice with a knife.

~)

Buried cables.
Downramp of water.
Fall's low angle of incidence.
Taut drive belts of factories, hazed and whirring buffalo.
Map lichen, thin explosion, high-hat gone solo,
rippling nine thousand years old.
Mouth, notch on a gun butt.
North Sask, cutting.

Horsechild's got the knack of floating like a rope
trailing behind a mare. This isn't mystical.
Just an effect of wind and the mind's
motion. He's blowing on grassfires
burning across the lines.

GRANDMOTHER

Maybe she does, weary, hang her prayers on the hooks of the house. Maybe she walks out. She ducks under the sheets darkening on the line, folds up the fields and tucks them in her bra. Beyond the yard light, she slips through the lilacs on the edge of the mown lawn and opens the door into a bear's shoulder. Her thick hair falls from her pearl barrettes and everything damp shivers close, the pulp of berries, rafts of roots, hot smell of undertracks. She could go back, but doesn't. The pasture sways under her feet, wilder than she remembers, the crashing waves of weeds, the smoke-film drift-leaves.

She sleeps days in a rusted-out car parked in the deepest grass, until she wears it like an almost see-through dress. Her hair loose, undone, her oversize glasses keep sliding down. She's rolling up her sleeves so birds can feed on her wrists. She might, she just might be talking to herself or to the other dead, learning to carve stories into teeth, learning to make sandals out of bark. She eats the fat. With a steady hand, she presses leaves in the only book of her thighs. In the leafless hereto thereafter, she'll sail them onto our dehydrated tongues.

Maybe she drives miles. She's asylumed to back roads. She's loving the breeze, the soft-blur of the blow-by, the backseat of her car heaped with knitted scarves and mittens, her old violin, the leg bones of antelope, bison, and deer. She doesn't wait for someone else to take her here or there. She doesn't kill the barn rats or balance the books. She doesn't bite her tongue or hide what she could have said on the backs of envelopes folded in her underwear drawer. She goes to coffee with the wind-worn. They talk the good poverty of boats. They talk dust and where-to-now. In her purse she's stashed pill bottles filled with the seven hundred varieties of corn, seeds of the bird's-eye view, the forgotten languages, the if-only. She hands out bowls of broth dug from the hilltops. She mails her notes to the wayward. She's good on gravel and black ice. She's full-up everafter gliding on empty.

She parks the wrong way on a one-way, rolls down the window, and waves him over. The reverb of a held note eddies off the shop fronts. With a flick of her wrist, she fans a handful of twenties, says pick a card, any card. Of the world, of the grassdunes, her smile is sun-bleached. She winks. Small birds lift to bare branches. He slings his sax on his back, says, It's you. She says, Get in. They drink whisky like it's a wind in the saplings. They shell peas. They listen to the little piano of the rain, its good right hand, its coming down. He curls up on the bench seat, legs too long, head on her lap. Migrating birds rest on the hood of their broken-down, their not-moving. And she combs the voices out like the burrs in his hair. Peace now, weather is weeping. Ride this continent out onto the dark seas.

LETTER TO KITTY, NEVER WRITTEN

A few errors have crept into my calculations.
Leaving on the next boat.
Forgive the scrawl.

Along with fifty pounds,
a lock of my hair.
Divide it in two.
Save half for the child,
fasten what's left to your own dark hair.

LONG AFTER LEAVING, BEING OVERTAKEN WITH THE CONSEQUENCES OF SUFFERING IN THE NORTHWEST

Wake, trying to wake, an ocean disced open between us, wind-drunk
fetch across the brine, weak-eyed and bundled into the bottom
of a canoe even in my sickbed, fireweed high, tipping
into the sun bearing down, smoothbored as a trade musket,
sour medicine of milky light sopping into the keeling room.
Drift, the unaiming drift of the needle, the canoe,
half-inch of freeboard. Headache, stupor, a dead pain.

Pray for a headwind, a bitch of a gale
to grind my teeth into.

Leaking? Is it leaking?

LETTER TO KITTY, NEVER WRITTEN

I've sat up the whole night
as if to watch you sleep as the sun
swings into the downwind
judder of the river,
gone river.

Can you hear it still,
a string loosened
to its most husky
silt-laden tone?

LETTER TO KITTY, NEVER WRITTEN

Athabasca, your dark hair,
dark hair of your sexual breathing,
your oilsweet hills, still burning.
In my hands, your smell,
the knifehandle of your smell.

LETTER TO KITTY, NEVER WRITTEN

Your belly, a swan's muscled body
shot out of the wind. I left you
a hatchet, cracked heels,
landslide in your cramping gut.
Did you make it back to your father's camp?

I'm thinner
now, untied, barely
walking, without guns.
Each day a star drifts one degree.

Are those your tracks
through the starving times?

LETTER TO KITTY, NEVER WRITTEN

You tend three birds dropped in your calm aim.
Strong meat, fire kindled in a split rock.
Do you carry a feathered purse?

You're not weeping?
Why won't you weep?

Why can't one of us simply weep?

LETTER TO KITTY, NEVER WRITTEN

I drowned long ago. I drowned in that country.

DUSK

In the dusk hour, the siphoned hour, the jawbone-sheened hour,
aspen hover like moths, they draw near, smooth-winged

and watery. When I lie down, trussed, drinking song
in their tilting, long-limbed and floating, on my back

in the lapping tracks, low-watt blue flames lift
what's passed—prairie grizzly, buffalo, black-footed

ferret, little curlew, small white lady's-slipper. The missing
have gone missing. Can someone at least say this?

When I lie down without closing my eyes,
darkness swells with leaf hiss, swells

like the ploughed, loose-haired seas—Bay of Bengal,
Solomon Sea, the Chukchi Sea—curling on doorsteps.

I am hinged at the lips. Somewhere a shelf of ice breaks off,
trails a wake of pebbles, little wheels spinning out.

Can I say my brother, too, is missing?

Though we haven't yet called the police.
When he rests his head, his good ear listens to concrete.

The cold walks in through the gates of his bones.
If this were a prayer, I would ask for the aspen

to quiet him like a blanket. No, ask for a wool blanket.
No. I'd ask him to rise and keep walking, though it's dark

and wind sirens in our ears. This darkness is
and is not of our choosing. The aspen glow, lanterns

after they've been put out, a coyote scalds tracks
in the frosted grass. Lightly we are tethered here.

WINDBOUND, UNNAMED CAMP

62° 54' 56" N
104° 44' 08" W

Hard-breathing hooves of the dark-hooded wind skid us sideways
across the river's buck, plough us to shore and the lowgrade crawl
to a backside hummock of shelter where wind digs us into the ground.
A merlin turns the screw in our ears.
Stutter before-the-brakes-blow, the pounding slow-mo bulldoze,
even the leashed boats threatening lift off, we fill them with stones.
Wind wheel-locks our sleep into big, crashing swells,
groundwater recharge from distant hills.
And I wake to put the voices back under the stones.

～⊃

Now the little bells carried in your fingers smaller than thorns.
Now the weight of your pack lifted again and again
from the carousel of the hills.
Now the weather of cover songs and reruns.
Now the old fashions, the gauzy blouse.
Now the wind that puts a hammer in hand, nails in your teeth,
and gives you nothing to bang together.

Light, a choir in the church basement leaking up through the floorboards,
the ankle-deep snowlight of the coming snow that comes before the snow.

The river rolls the credits for none of this.

400 km from any settlement, we float the raft of our flagging
civilization on plans for getting out. We size up the depth
and width of the river, taxi distance of a Twin.
Could we get a plane down here?

Now the parachute of the river fails over your shoulders.
Now the eyes of the boulders buoy you up.
Now the eyes like bullets caught in the teeth.
Now snow slants in, fake money.
Now skin from the heels of walking long.

~⌒

Wind herds its meat through our chests and our voices no longer
live in our throats. And the wind's flanks sweat the smell
of the people-far-to-the-other-side, people-of-the-rebounding-
hills north of the lake that floats driftwood, and further east,
people-of-the-place-that-lies-across who pulled whitefish
from the crooked lake, the grassy shores oceaned briefly with geese,
sweat of the people-who-never-returned after so many starved in '58
when the caribou veered somewhere not here, people-from-the-place-
where-the-sun-follows-east-to-west, whirlpools-aplenty-
people on the lower river of the swift little fish, who moved below
the lake of white swans, sweat of the people-who-have-cooking-pots
on the great fish river, sweat of the coast-dwellers-where-bones-abound,
sweat of the many people-of-the-willow, the out-of-the-way-dwellers north
of the big river, sweat of the people-from-beyond, the dwellers-of-the-flat-
land-people, the bedrock-people.

This is a wind to be buried in.

~)

This is where he walks down from the shuffle of uneasy hills,
cheapo guitar on his back, brings smoke trailing the whiplines of water.

He dangles hooks in the rise of lost voices.
He's snagging stones by their soft mouths.

He talks low to himself or to wolves over the horizon that's just over
the horizon and whistles the teeth down, dice in our hands
we shake and shake, but never throw.

~⌒

J.W. Tyrrell, 1900, carries a sextant with a folding mercurial horizon,
one solar compass, two pocket compasses, two prismatic compasses,
one fluid compass, two boat logs, two clinometers,
one aneroid barometer, a thermometer, a chronometer,
three good watches, field glasses, aluminum binoculars, and a camera
across the Keewatin barrens for the Dominion Land Survey.
He cuts the sleeves off his borrowed caribou coat,
binds them over his bloody feet.
Walks alone now still mapping the jagged contours of the lake
where silence is the only animal that limps alongside his muttering.
His maps, small flames sputtering on his palm.

Now the smoke of nowhere to go gets in your eyes.
Now you have a map and the map is sleeting curtains of dusk.
Now take the hair that is offered, wear it over your back.

Tyrell lies down in the lee behind a boulder,
rain soaks him through.
Silence: the map you are making
when you don't know where you are.

And further north in a stand of beyond-the-treeline spruce,
Edgar Christian, 1927, eighteen years old, hauls
the bodies of Hornby and Adlard out of a cabin.
The caribou have not come this way.
He puts his diary in the ashes of the cold stove, stumbles
back to the slab of his bed, his legs dangling over the edge.
He has sipped his last meal, boiled broth from the skins
of an animal trapped two months ago and dug from the snow.
He crawls after the wind-sound in the stovepipe to see

snow turning to blue sea swell, wind's prow
bearing down its cargo of nights.

The spruce give their dark robes away,
the river, its rack of antlers stampeding by,
his tongue in the ashes of the cold stove.

~ ⁀

Now 400 km in every direction inside the combine of the wind.
Now the wait-it-out of the ribcage, the shuddering tent fly.
Now the clanging buckets of the sky weigh down our arms.
The caribou are not here only because they are not here
and urgent the wind rises with the muscle of two bulls, locked,
bloody strips of velvet weeks ago flung to the roaring ground.

No, he's not speaking to me, still
not speaking. He's not saying
where he'll find the spoon for the bowl
he pulls out of his hood.

I ask why he's taking off his coat in this weather.

Coat of smoke.
Coat of decay in the core of the ropes.
Coat of diagnosis.
Coat of refusal of diagnosis.
Coat of staying too long in one place.
Coat of always moving.
Coat of the little helpless mirrors of the snow, sweet crude
slowed in the cold, thick mane of nowhere to go.
Coat of tracks blown in by the wind.

If his path is the path of cast-off coats, unprotected
from the weather, if he trades empties
for boots of running water, if he transcribes wolf
riffs on the back of bank receipts
in the tiniest scrawl, the whole map
of how to get here fits in the book of his walk.

Stars screw into the roof of his skull.

He leans his head against the payphone,
holds the receiver out to the wind.

— *Thelon River*

TLOGOTSHO—BIG PLACE OF GRASS

61° 11' 12" N
124° 30' 59" W

Above the treeline on the knuckled ridges of the sprawled plateau,
laid down like a worked hand, I was walking off
grief, walking the high muskeg, the rim
of a glacial lake that once filled the valley, where now
the river, a stranger, 1,500 metres below, took my picture.
If I had it still, you could see I'd almost disappeared.
You could see the plateau, its squarish sail, an afterlife
looming, but taking on a hazy cyanosis
as light turned its shoulder.
The lake, ten thousand or so years away.
Our last phone call not quite disconnected.
I was walking far behind Barry and John.
Heavy pack, tippy boulders,
Dall lambs already running at top speed,
owning the high country. We took down
one hunting blind, scattered the stones,
walked through jet trails and the thin slips of streams.

— *South Nahanni River*

DOUBLE-BARREL LAKE

62° 34' 04" N
104° 50' 07" W

Bed down in the northern lights, in the fat spoor
of a solar wind, mattress of its swaying boughs.
Sky's black roaring of the retina,
somatosensory cortex spools out to lick
all you think you've seen.
Bed down in the crawl space called *is*,
called *this*, film of your senses thin-ribboned
between ground and sky,
the blown eye. Heart,
eye's blackness
on which light moves.

— *Thelon River*

THE SPLITS

61° 07' 25" N
123° 36' 31" W

Last camp before the mountains fall behind.
Figure on the river's shifty nature, slipshod delta
weave, dragonfly, but with the big shoulders and a janitor's
jangling keys. River splits into its dicey nighthawks
strumming warm air rising off cobble beaches.
Braided, settling, river still teethed
to undercut the outside bank.
All our wet clothes hung on willows.
The loose lug nuts of a fall wind.
Waterline dropping.
The Butte's got its squat woodstove stoked,
the spiny fins of the front range zipline away.
Peter throttles down and waves,
headed upstream for a moose, packed light,
thermos, gun, and a couple gas cans,
he'll sleep in the bottom of his boat.
We're one day from flying out.

—— *South Nahanni River*

NOTES

The Mackenzie poems grew out of my reading of *The Journals and Letters of Sir Alexander Mackenzie*, edited by W. Kaye Lamb (Cambridge, University Press, 1970). Mackenzie (1764–1820) does not discuss his dreams in his journals, but two letters that he wrote during the winter of 1794 to his cousin Roderic Mackenzie briefly mention his deep depression, his visions of the dead, and his determination to get out of the Athabasca country for good.

The death of "the Catt, Sir Alexander Mackenzie's wife" is recorded in the 1804 journal kept at Fort Chipewyan. Mackenzie likely married the Catt *à la façon du pays* when he was in his early twenties, two to four years before his expedition down the Deh Cho, and spent up to ten years in a relationship with her. He never mentions her in his own journals, but in one letter, sent from a ship leaving North America to his cousin in the Northwest, he writes: "I requested of you at parting to send fifty pounds to Mrs. Mackenzie of Three Rivers on my account . . .This sum I mean to continue to her annually while Kitty remains Single."

In "Mackenzie's Dream," the line "On the third day of hunger it is hard to walk far or fast enough to kill" is quoted from *Maps and Dreams* (Douglas & McIntyre, 1981) by Hugh Brody.

"The Limits of Travel in This Direction" is influenced by eyewitness accounts, from Helge Ingstad, Chick Ferguson, and Father Antoine Binamé, of the "Great Flu" of 1928 in the Mackenzie District as recorded in René Fumoleau's book *As Long As This Land Shall Last: A History of Treaty 8 and Treaty 11, 1870–1939* (University of Calgary Press, 2004).

Maria Campbell's *Maclean's* article "She Who Knows the Truth of Big Bear" (September 1975) recounts See-as-cum-ka-poo's memories of her husband, Horsechild, who was twelve years old when he was sent to residential school after his father, Big Bear, the great Cree chief who tried to negotiate peace and justice for his starving people, was imprisoned for treason. See-as-cum-ka-poo, also known as Mary PeeMee, was close to one hundred years old at the time of the interview and living on the Poundmaker Reserve.

The Inuktitut name "Nadlok" can be translated as "place where the deer cross." In 1985–86, the Canadian Museum of Civilization unearthed more than forty thousand caribou bone segments and many artifacts on this tiny island. Bryan Gordon's report "Nadlok and the Origin of the Copper Inuit," found on the museum's website, suggests that this site was occupied between 1450 and 1750 when ocean temperatures dropped, the seal population crashed, and coastal peoples moved inland to rely on the caribou.

In *Arctic Dreams* (Bantam, 1986), Barry Lopez compares the journals of a number of explorers and notes that "the description of the land in an early report affects the description of the same landscape in a later report," a quotation that I have altered slightly in "Map Unrolled on the Table."

Physicist James Trefil reports that "the average river requires a million years to move a grain of sand one hundred inches."

"Windbound, Unnamed Camp" adapts the English translations of the names of the following peoples whose traditional lands span the tundra east of Hudson's Bay, the area today known as the Kivalliq Region of Nunavut: Akilinirmiut, Hanningajurmiut (also called Ualininmiut), Harvaqtuurmiut, Utkusiksalinmiut, Hauniqtuurmiut, Paatlirmiut,

Ahiarmiut, Ihalmiut, Qairnirmiut. The translations are adapted from "Tuhaalruuqtut Ancestral Sounds" by the Baker Lake Inuit Heritage Centre found at www.virtualmuseum.ca.

The list of instruments J. W. Tyrell carried across the Keewatin District is lifted from his memoir *Across the Sub-arctics of Canada* (W. Briggs, 1908).

Edgar Christian's diary, originally published under the title *Unflinching* (J. Murray, 1937), has been reissued as *Death in the Barren Ground* (Oberon, 1980).

The Dené Tha name "Tlogotsho" can be translated as "big place of grass."

As Earth is not a perfect sphere, different map datums estimate its shape and size in different ways. The coordinates here use the World Geodetic System (WGS 84), the current standard for navigation by satellite, which is based on an ellipsoid calculated from Earth's centre of mass.

ACKNOWLEDGEMENTS

I am grateful for financial support from: the Saskatchewan Arts Board, the Social Sciences and Humanities Research Council, the University of Victoria Humanities Interdisciplinary Fellowship, the President's Research Scholarship, the Howard E. Petch Research Scholarship, the Millen Graduate Award, the Centre for Studies in Religion and Society, and the Ian H. Stewart Graduate Fellowship.

In 2008 I travelled on the Athabasca River through the tar sands with members of the Keepers of the Athabasca. I am grateful to the elders and youth at the Keepers of the Water gatherings in Fort Chipewyan and in many communities along the Athabasca who shared their stories. Thanks also to Glenn Patterson and Mike Mercredi. And to all the keepers of the water.

My deep thanks to Tim Lilburn, Lorna Crozier, and Patrick Lane— wise teachers, steady guides, always. Thank you to Anne-Marie Turza for rich conversation, fine edits, and for travelling with me into the poems. And thanks to Ken Babstock, who edited the manuscript with acuity.

Thanks to Ellen Seligman and Anita Chong and everyone at McClelland & Stewart for your first-rate work on this project, for making it possible.

And for support in many tangible and intangible ways, thanks to Nicol Lischka, Sue Gee, Barb Henderson, Valerie Tenning, Paul Bramadat, and Neil Hartling. I have warm memories of all the people who have paddled these rivers with me.

All my love to Rob Skelly, my paddling partner on the North Saskatchewan and many rivers to come. And to my family—we carry on together.

My love and respect to the rivers.